THE MEDITERRANEAN DIET FOR BEGINNERS

An Easy & Complete Guide for Food Lovers to Burn Fat Fast, Lose

Weight and Stay Healthy

Caterina Di Marco

THE MEDITERRANEAN DIET FOR BEGINNERS

Copyright © 2021 by Caterina Di Marco All rights reserved.

ISBN Paperback: 978-1-80157-225-5

Printed by IngramSpark

First printing edition 2021.

Table of Content

INTRODUCTION

Understanding What the Mediterranean Diet IsThere really is no single, all-encompassing definition of the Mediterranean diet. The term itself was coined to describe the tasty cuisines eaten by natives of the countries who share the Mediterranean Sea as a common border. As a matter of fact, the Mediterranean diet is normally identified by the presence of fruits, vegetables, beans, whole grains, nuts, olive oil, and seeds.

Here are the main features of Mediterranean diet plans:

- ➤ Healthy fats, whole grains, fruits, and veggies are all consumed on a day-to-day basis.
- ➤ Food items measured by the week include poultry, fish, eggs, and beans.
- ➤ Dairy products are taken moderately.
- ➤ The intake of red meat is highly monitored and limited.

There are, of course, other equally important features of the Mediterranean diet. They include physical activities, meal sharing with friends and loved ones, and the tantalizing option of downing a glass of red wine.

A Predominantly Plant-Based Diet

The Mediterranean diet is primarily based on veggies, herbs, nuts, beans, whole grains, and fruits. All meals are prepared to reflect this important pillar. Also important to the proper implementation of the diet are moderate servings of poultry, dairy, eggs, and seafood. In stark contrast to this, red meat is only consumed once in a while.

Presence of Recommended Fats

Fats, the healthy types, are another important feature of the Mediterranean diet. They are consumed in place of unhealthy fats such as trans and saturated fats. Those ones are largely known to cause heart problems in humans.

The basic source of healthy fats in the Mediterranean diet plan is Olive oil. Olive oil produces a good amount of the type of fat referred to as monounsaturated. This fat reduces the body's total

THE MEDITERRANEAN DIET FOR BEGINNERS
intake of cholesterol, as well as bad cholesterol.

Monounsaturated fats can equally be found in nuts and seeds, all predominant features of the Mediterranean diet.

The importance of fish to the Mediterranean diet cannot be overstated. Fatty fish contain a high level of Omega-3 fatty acids. Working in the body as polyunsaturated fat, Omega-3 fatty acids can help you lower the body's inflammation level, help eliminate blood clotting, reduce triglycerides. All of these serve to substantially protect the body from the possibility of a stroke or heart failure. Examples of fatty fishes perfect for your Mediterranean diet are herring, mackerel, albacore tuna, sardines, lake trout, and salmon.

Where Does the Wine Come In?

Although the Mediterranean diet allows you to indulge in red wine, it is typically done to a measured moderation. Just because some studies have linked a lower risk of heart ailments to alcohol does not automatically give an all-clear. As stated in the Dietary Guidelines for Americans, caution should be applied when venturing into drinking or increasing one's drinking limits to reap some rewards health-wise.

This is why the Mediterranean diet is centered basically on increasing your intake of wholesomely fresh food items and boosting engagement in physical activities and sharing meals with your loved ones. Together, all three elements form the famed Pyramid of the Mediterranean Diet. When properly done, they can have a real impact on your physical and mental health and help you find pleasure in consuming tasty, healthier foods.

What Are The Health Benefits of a Mediterranean Diet?

It goes without saying that our health is significantly impacted by what we consume. It is not only telling on our overall health status but also our brain health. Being on a diet plan that suits your body can boost your thinking ability, aid memory, and information processing as you go about your daily activities.

> ➢ **It helps reduce the possibility of cardiovascular disease.**

Ample evidence proves that the Mediterranean diet can help lessen the risk of contracting a cardiovascular ailment. A particular study compared a couple of Mediterranean diets with one other controlled diet for about five years. At the end of the research, it was discovered that the Mediterranean diet had lowered the risk of cardiovascular ailments by at least 30% when compared with the other controlled diet. Despite this, further studies will be required to prove whether or not certain lifestyle variables like physical engagements and viable social support systems impact the reduced rate of lower heart problems as found in the Mediterranean region, compared to the United States.

> ➢ **Helps You Sleep Better**

In 2018, some researchers decided to explore the Mediterranean diet's effects on the quality of sleep.

The conclusion of their studies proved that proper implementation of the Mediterranean diet can indeed help increase the quality of sleep in older adults. It also showed that the Mediterranean diet has no such effect on younger individuals.

> **Maintains Your Agility**

As an individual in the adult category, some of the nutritional values profited from implementing a Mediterranean diet could lower the risk of your body muscles weakening and several other body frailty symptoms by at least 70%.

> **Lowers the Possibility of Developing Alzheimer's.**

Since research has shown that the Mediterranean diet can help better your blood sugar levels, cholesterol, and generally, the health of your blood vessel levels; it could help lower the possibility of developing Alzheimer's or even dementia.

> ➢ **Reduces the Possibility of Parkinson's Disease by Half.**

The Mediterranean diet contains a rather high component of antioxidants. This can help combat the damage of cells (also referred to as oxidative stress) and significantly reduce Parkinson's.

> ➢ **Boosts Your Longevity.**

With the risks of developing potentially fatal diseases like heart problems or even cancer significantly lowered, a Mediterranean diet automatically reduces an individual's chances of dying by at least twenty percent.

> ➢ **Combats Diabetes of The Type 2 Variety**

The presence of a high constituent of fiber, which aids slow digestion, helps to prevent serious blood sugar fluctuations, and keep your weight stable and healthy.

> ➢ **Weight loss**

THE MEDITERRANEAN DIET FOR BEGINNERS

For individuals interested in losing weight, the Mediterranean diet is a great dietary and lifestyle option to help them achieve their body goals.

Mediterranean Diet: The Myths and The Facts

Now you know just how loaded with health benefits the Mediterranean diet is, but it is quite worrying how many popular misconceptions there are on a diet, the lifestyle and how it leads to a more healthy and extended life. In this section, we'll look at some of the most common misconceptions about the Mediterranean diet.

Mediterranean Myths & Facts

Myth One: *The Mediterranean Lifestyle is expensive to maintain.*

Fact: This myth is just as sad as it is funny. Following a Mediterranean diet means you're cooking your meals with the likes of lentils and beans as your primary protein source. You're also using fundamentally with more plant-based sources as well as whole grains. Factually, living like this is way less expensive than indulging in processed and/or packaged foods.

Myth Two: *Since a glass of wine does the heart some good, three should be thrice as healthy.*

Fact: *It is true that wine, consumed moderately, is good for the heart. In this case, moderate consumption is limited to two glasses for men daily and just one for women. This can have a greatly positive impact on your health. That said, going beyond this limit is actually dangerous to your health.*

Myth 3: *The Mediterranean diet is typified by consuming extravagant quantities of pasta and bread daily.*

Fact: *On the contrary, the Mediterranean, on whose eating habits the diet is named after, does not consume large portions of pasta like some Americans like to do. As a matter of fact, the Mediterranean use pasta of about half a cup to a cup serving as a form of side dish. Their plate is mostly filled with veggies, salads,* organic (grass-fed) meat in little portions, fish, and maybe one

paltry slice of bread.

Myth 4: *Food is the sole component of the Mediterranean diet.*

Fact*: Food indeed forms a significant portion of the*

Mediterranean diet, but the Mediterranean's other lifestyle habits

are equally important and cannot be overlooked. A lot can be

learned from how the Mediterranean eat their meals. For example,

they don't eat in a hurry or in the form of television. They usually

eat relaxed and in a leisurely mood. They also make it a point of

eating with others, not alone. The people of the Mediterranean

region also place a lot of emphasis on physical activities. These

lifestyle habits are just as vital to your health status as what you

put on your plate to eat.

Disadvantages of the Mediterranean Diet

➤ **Your Milk Intake Is Moderated**

Eating the Mediterranean diet poses no real long-term risks, as proved by various academic research conclusions. But if you happen to be a huge fan of milk or milk is your primary source of calcium, you might be slightly put off by the diet. It's not like you won't get to eat your yogurt and cheese, but you'll now be doing so in limited rations.

To get your fill of calcium without milk, you'll need to consume plenty of yogurt and cheese or explore non-dairy sources like sardines, fortified almond milk, tofu prepared with calcium and sulfate, or kale.

Alternatively, you could simply drink skim milk.

➤ **You Have to Place A Cap on Alcohol Consumption.**

What makes the Mediterranean diet perhaps unique is that it sees the social consumption of red wine as a healthy activity. But that only remains so as long as you don't stray away from the recommended limits of two glasses and one for men and women, respectively.

Also, if your family has a history of breast cancer, then you must be aware that alcohol consumption increases the risk significantly. You should have a conversation with your doctor to see what's proper for you in such a case.

> **Like Wine, Fat Is Also Rationed**

It is true that you only consume healthy fats in the Mediterranean diet plan, yet it also true that even good things can be overused or abused. Although the Mediterranean diet fully meets the standard requirements for saturated fats intake (as confirmed by the American Heart Association), you could potentially take your consumption above the amount of fat recommended per day if you don't pay enough attention to your intake. The required daily amount is capped at 65 g per day.

➤ **You Have to Make Time to Cook.**

Cooking is a huge part of the Mediterranean diet. Granted, you won't need to spend tons of hours sweating in the kitchen, but you will definitely be cooking because the emphasis is on tasty, fresh meals. You can even use the opportunity to improve your culinary skills and achieve valuable milestones.

➤ **Developing A Mediterranean Diet**

Being a plant-based lifestyle, the Mediterranean diet places premium emphasis on foods derived from plant sources, more than most diets out there. It is not strange to find a meal comprising legumes, veggies, and whole grains in a particular Mediterranean diet meal plan.

Followers of the Mediterranean diet basically prepare their meals using plenty of spices and healthy fats like olive oil. Their meals also often include a moderate amount of meat, eggs, or fish.

Red wine (moderate amounts), sparkling water, and, of course, water are the normal choice of drinks.

Food to Eat

This issue of which particular foods should make up part of the Mediterranean diet has been a controversial source in the past. This is because the diet varies from country to country.

However, certain Mediterranean foods do not court controversy, and they are really what your diet should be based upon.

They include:

> - **Veggies**: Kale, cucumbers, onions, spinach, cauliflower, tomatoes, Brussels sprouts, broccoli, carrots, etc.
> - **Fruits**: Oranges, strawberries, peaches, figs, bananas, dates, apples, pears, melons, etc.
> - **Nuts and seeds:** Hazelnuts, Pumpkin seeds, hazelnuts, walnuts, sunflower seeds, cashews, almonds, macadamia nuts, etc.
> - **Legumes**: Chickpeas, lentils, peanuts, peas, beans, pulses, etc.
> - **Tubers**: Yams, sweet potatoes, potatoes, turnips, etc.

➤ **Whole grains:** Pasta, buckwheat, brown rice, whole grain bread, rye, corn, barley, whole oats, etc.

➤ **Fish and seafood:** Sardines, tuna, crab, shrimp, trout, mackerel, salmon, clams, mussels, oysters, etc.

➤ **Poultry**: Turkey, chicken, duck.

➤ **Eggs**: Quail, duck eggs, chicken.

➤ **Dairy**: Yogurt, cheese, Greek yogurt, etc.

➤ **Herbs and spices:** Pepper, nutmeg, mint, sage, garlic, cinnamon, Basil, rosemary, etc.

➤ **Healthy Fats:** Avocados, olives, olive oil, avocado oil.

➤ Central to the success of your Mediterranean diet plan are single/whole ingredient foods.

Water should be your go-to beverage on a Mediterranean diet. On the choice of drinks, water should be your ideal choice on a Mediterranean diet.

The Mediterranean diet also includes moderate consumption of red wine. However, this part of the diet is optional, not essential.

Ordinarily, wine should not be indulged in by individuals who are alcoholic.

Tea and coffee can be condoned in a Mediterranean diet, but the likes of fruit juices and beverages contain excessively high sugar content and should be strictly avoided.

Food to Avoid on A Mediterranean Diet

Individuals who are on the Mediterranean diet are to stay away from the following foods:

- **Refined grains** like white pasta, pizza dough, white bread.
- **Refined oils** like soybean oil and canola oil.
- **Foods that contain added sugars** like sodas, pastries, and candies should also be avoided.
- **Processed meats** in general, like hot dogs and deli meats, are also not recommended.
- Any kind of packaged or processed foods.

THE MEDITERRANEAN DIET FOR BEGINNERS

As pointed out earlier, the Mediterranean diet is a combination of eating lifestyles of the different countries that share the Mediterranean Sea as a border. This makes it difficult to find one single definitely or description of the diet.

We can only say that the diet is a lifestyle that is centered around the consumption of plant-based food sources and a very low intake of animal foods. The diet also focuses its meat intake on seafood and fish.

The internet is a big library of information on the Mediterranean diet, with many books on the subject globally.

To improve the quality of your health, especially where the heart is concerned, lose weight consistently and cultivate healthy eating habits that will leave help your body grow, you might want to give the Mediterranean diet a chance.

Clearly, the Mediterranean diet isn't one of these food diets making the rounds on the internet today. It has definitely been around for centuries, has been the way of life of the

Mediterranean for longer than you can imagine.

Due to its long stay, there's been enough time to prove its effects,

ranging from reducing the possibility of developing certain

diseases to loss of weight and increasing brain function.

Regardless of all these, you won't find it easy to be consistent

with a diet without satisfying and challenging. This is exactly

what the Mediterranean diet is. The recipes are refreshing, filled

with flavor, and straight out of the farm. You will even find

certain combinations you perhaps haven't come across before

(say earthy mushrooms with nutty tahini, lamb sausage with

preserved lemons, pomegranate molasses with straight from the

farm halloumi cheese, etc.).

However, it is important to point out that saying the recipes are

fresh or modern isn't to say the ingredients are not realistic for a

modest home. Some of the names which might sound rare (some

spices like harissa, za'atar, and sumac) have been carefully

explained, how to get them and where.

THE MEDITERRANEAN DIET FOR BEGINNERS

This section will help you in your shopping for your staple products. Existing flavors like lemons, garlic, and herbs also find new powerful roles in these recipes.

The aim is to simplify these meals to be easy to prepare and not considered weekend events due to time constraints and other factors.

Despite this, all meals retain their nutritional values, catering to your taste buds, and helping you find more enjoyment in life.

PART ONE: BREAKFASTS

MEAL 1: BACON, ZUCCHINI, & FETTA FRITTERS (& AVOCADO SALSA)

Ingredients

- ✓ Two finely chopped middle bacon rashers.

- ✓ Two coarsely grated zucchinis.

- ✓ A third of a cup of flour (self-raising variety)

- ✓ An egg whisked gently. ⅓ cup self-rising flour

- ✓ Vegetable oil

- ✓ Two hundred grams of crumbled Lemnos Smooth Fetta.

- ✓ A tablespoon of chopped dill, coarsely done.

- ✓ A tablespoon of lime juice

- ✓ Two hundred and fifty grams of cherry tomatoes are divided into two.

- ✓ A piece of ripe avocado divided into two, free of stone and chopped coarsely.

- ✓ Lime wedges

- ✓ Two tablespoons of chives chopped roughly.

Preparations

To prepare the salsa:

1. Mix the tomatoes, lime juice, and avocados inside a medium-sized bowl.

2. With the back of your spoon, crush the mixture lightly.

3. Then join the chives and one half of the Fetta to the bowl's contents and combine them by tossing gently.

Fritters preparations:

1. First, you have to get a large frying pan. Set the heat to medium and cook the bacon over it.

2. Cook for about five minutes or until it turns crisp, stirring all the way.

3. Next, remove the bacon and put it on a plate already laced with a paper towel.

4. Squeeze out liquid (with your hands) from the zucchini, as much as possible. Then put it in a big bowl. Join the flour, egg, dill, and bacon to it, and mix them together by stirring.

5. Next, include the other half of the Fetta and stir diligently to make sure they mix well.

6. Set your heat to medium and set a large frying pan over it to heat the oil.

7. Using a spoon, spread a fourth of a cup of the already mixed zucchini all over the pan. Cook until it turns golden brown; that should take about two minutes max.

8. Cook for another two to three minutes, turning intermittently until it changes to a golden-brown color and feels crispy. Then move to a paper towel-lined plate.

9. Go over the same procedure with what's left of the mixture. That should take about two further batches.

10. When serving the meal, place the fritters, topped with lime wedges and avocado salsa, into serving plates.

MEAL 2: TORTILLA CRUNCHIES WITH BREAKFAST EGGS

Ingredients

- ✓ Four tortillas (soft)

- ✓ Two huge handfuls of washed baby spinach (leaves).

- ✓ Eight, cut into quarters, cherry tomatoes.

- ✓ Six lightly beaten fresh eggs.

- ✓ Just grounded black pepper and sea salt.

- ✓ One hundred and eighty grams of crumbled Lemnos Fetta (traditional)

- ✓ Olive oil (spray)

Preparation:

1. Your oven must be preheated at a heat level of 170°C.

2. Get four large ovenproof ramekins (of about ten centimeters) and spray them with olive oil. Then soften the tortillas by microwaving them for a couple of seconds.

3. Next, line the ramekins and tortillas carefully in the oven and bake them for about seven to ten minutes. When you feel them starting to crisp up, remove them from the oven.

4. Meanwhile, as the cases of tortillas bake in the oven, pour boiling hot water into the spinach. This will make it wilt.

5. Drain the water immediately, chop roughly, and put it aside.

6. In a large bowl, mix the eggs, cherry tomatoes, crumbled Fetta, and chopped blanched spinach. Season with salt and pepper.

7. Divide the fetta and egg mix between the tortillas, cover with foil and bake for 20-25 minutes or until the eggs are cooked through.

8. Serve warm for breakfast or brunch.

MEAL 3: ROSTI WITH FETTA CREAM

DRESSING AND SALMON

Ingredients

- ✓ Three tablespoons of sour cream (light)

- ✓ One hundred grams of Lemnos smooth Fetta.

- ✓ Just grounded black pepper and sea salt.

- ✓ A lone portion of freshly smoked salmon, with the entire skin, peeled off and flaked.

- ✓ Hundred grams of washed rocket leaves.

- ✓ Lemon wedges

- ✓ A piece of ripe avocado.

Rosti

- ✓ Seven hundred and fifty grams of waxy potatoes. Either of Nicola or Desiree is recommended, or any other similar variety you can find. They should be thoroughly scrubbed, then parboiled, and left to cool.

- ✓ An egg (beaten).

✓ Forty grams of melted butter.

Preparation

The dressing

1. Using a fork, beat the Fetta inside a medium-sized bowl.

2. Then mix the beaten Fetta with the sour cream and season accordingly with black pepper and sea salt.

3. Then cover and place in the refrigerator until you're ready to serve.

To make the Rosti

1. Peel the skins off the parboiled potatoes (should be easy), then shred or grate them.

2. Get a big bowl and bring together the well-beaten egg, shredded/grated potatoes, salt, pepper, and melted butter.

3. Place your frying pan over medium heat and pour the oil into the pan so that it's just about covering it.

4. Divide the mixture of potatoes into about eight equal cakes and, batch after batch, fry them all.

5. Using an egg flipper or a spatula, turn the cakes while you fry and make sure each side gets about three to four minutes each. Remove once it turns crispy and golden brown.

6. Drain each cake with paper towels and keep them in warmth until you're ready to eat.

7. When serving, put two Rosti in one plate and top each plate with avocado slices, freshly smoked salmon, rockets, and conclude with a lemon wedge, cream sauce, and fetta dollop.

MEAL 4: GREEK YOGURT WITH NUTS, FRUITS, HONEY, & CINNAMON

This is a simple dessert of Greek origins, made with Greek yogurt, honey, cinnamon, and walnuts. This treat is strictly gluten-free, vegetarian, no-baked, and highly proteinous.

Ingredients

- ✓ Half a cup of Greek yogurt
- ✓ One tablespoon of walnuts (crushed)
- ✓ Cinnamon as it suits your taste.
- ✓ A tablespoon of honey, to your taste if you so wish.

Preparation

1. Use a spoon to transfer the yogurt into a small-sized dessert dish
2. Add a sprinkling of crushed walnuts on the yogurt.
3. To bring out their natural flavor some more, you may decide to toast the walnuts gently in a hot skillet.

4. Sprinkle the yogurt with cinnamon and drizzle with honey.

5. Add a sprinkling of cinnamon to the yogurt and end the process with a drizzling of honey.

6. Serve to taste.

MEAL 5: CAPRESE AVOCADO TOAST

Ingredients

- ✓ One piece of avocado

- ✓ One half of the juice from one half of a lemon.

- ✓ Just ground black pepper.

- ✓ Salt (Kosher)

- ✓ Two giant slices of toasted sourdough.

- ✓ Half cuttings of halved cherry tomatoes.

- ✓ 1 cup of mozzarella balls (i.e., Ciliegine)

- ✓ Flaky sea salt

- ✓ Two pieces of basil leaves, freshly sliced.

- ✓ For drizzling, you'll need Balsamic glaze.

Preparation

1. Get a large bowl, mash your avocado with a fork and mix with lemon juice. Then add salt and pepper seasoning.

2. Layer the mixture on toast and add cherry tomatoes and the mozzarellas as toppings.

3. Add a sprinkling of flaky sea salt, add a drizzling of balsamic glaze, and garnish with Basil.

4. Serve.

MEAL 6: GRAIN SALAD FOR BREAKFAST WITH HAZELNUTS, BLUEBERRIES, & LEMON

Ingredients

- ✓ A cup of golden quinoa (dried)

- ✓ A cup of oats (steel-cut)

- ✓ Half a cup of millet (dried)

- ✓ Three divided tablespoons of Olive oil.

- ✓ Two big lemons, juice, and zest.

✓ A piece of one-inched freshly peeled ginger. Sliced into coins.

✓ Half a cup of maple syrup.

✓ A quarter teaspoon of nutmeg.

✓ A cup of Greek yogurt. You can use soy vegan instead if you wish to make the meal vegan.

✓ Two cups of either Blueberries or mixed berries.

✓ Two cups of coarsely chopped and roasted hazelnuts.

Preparation

1. First, get a mesh strainer and mix the millet, oats, and quinoa inside. Then place beneath running water and rinse for up to sixty seconds. Then set it aside.

2. Next, get a saucepan (three-quart) and place it over medium heat.

3. Heat a tablespoon of olive oil in the saucepan and join the raised grains to it. Cook for about two to three minutes until you can perceive the smell of toast.

4. Pour in half a cup of water (four times), add a third of teaspoon salt, zest for one lemon and the ginger coins.

5. Cook until it boils, then turn down the heat and simmer for about twenty minutes.

6. Next, turn off your heat and allow it to sit idle for 5 minutes.

7. Take off the lid and using a fork, fluff it. Withdraw the ginger. Place hot grains over your big baking sheet and cool off for about thirty minutes.

8. Once the grains have cooled off, dish into a large bowl and add the other lemon's zest. Stir.

9. Using a medium-sized bowl, emulsify all two lemons' juice and the two tablespoons of olive oil remaining by whisking comprehensively.

10. Do the same with the maple syrup, nutmeg and yogurt, pour on the grains and stir until they're completely coated.

11. Add the blueberries and already toasted hazelnuts, stir. If needed, you can season with more salt.

12. Allow this mixture to remain in the fridge overnight. This

    will allow the flavors really interact and integrate properly.

MEAL 7: AVOCADO & EGG BREAKFAST

PIZZA

Ingredients

- ✓ A piece of Hass avocado (large)

- ✓ A tbsp of smoothly chopped cilantro

- ✓ A teaspoon and half of lime juice

- ✓ One-eighth tbsp of salt.

- ✓ Half a pound of store-bought or homemade pizza dough.

- ✓ Four big eggs.

- ✓ A tablespoons of vegetable oil.

- ✓ For serving, you might add hot sauce, although this is only

    if you want to.

Preparation

1. Divide the avocado into half its length. Extract the pit.

   With a huge spoon, transfer the flesh into a medium sized

bowl. Put the lime juice, salt and cilantro and mash until it becomes smooth, using a fork. Add a couple of chunks of avocado and mash some more. *The size of the avocado you use will determine how much salt or lime you'll add.* Set this aside.

2. Portion the dough into four equal sizes. Using a cutting board that has been properly floured, roll each into a circle just about 6-inches thin. If the dough won't stop springing back in your face as you attempt to roll it, let it rest for a while. Try again once the gluten is sufficiently relaxed.

3. Take a properly seasoned iron cast skillet and heat over medium heat till it turns hot. Put a dough circle in the middle of the skillet and cook for a couple of minutes until you can see that the surface is bubbly and the bottom is sufficiently browned. Then flip over and cook the other side as well, until it's browned too. Hold the dough down with a spatula since the dough is likely to puff off the underside of the pan. Transfer the completed circle to a

plate and go over the same process with each of the

remaining circles.

4. Take a quarter of the avocado mixture and spread on each

   of the already cooked dough piece.

5. You'll need to heat your oil in a skillet. If you intend to use

   the same skillet, you need to let it cool, then clean out

   residue flour that may have clung to it. Fry your eggs to

   desired taste and place on each pizza. You may serve

   immediately, whether or not you drizzle hot sauce on it.

If you don't happen to have the cast iron skillet needed, you can

make use of a stainless-steel variety. In this case you'll have to add

a very light layer of oil to the pan before proceeding to cook the

pizzas.

MEAL 8: SPINACH ARTICHOKE FRITTATA

Ingredients

- ✓ 10 large eggs

- ✓ 1/2 cup full-fat sour cream

- ✓ 1 tablespoon Dijon mustard

- ✓ 1 teaspoon kosher salt

- ✓ 1/4 teaspoon freshly ground black pepper

- ✓ 1 cup grated Parmesan cheese (about 3 ounces), divided

- ✓ 2 tablespoons olive oil

- ✓ About 14 ounces marinated artichoke hearts, drained, patted dry, and quartered

- ✓ 5 ounces baby spinach (about 5 packed cups)

- ✓ 2 cloves garlic, minced

Preparation

1. Arrange a rack in the middle of the oven and heat to 400°F.

2. Place the eggs, sour cream, mustard, salt, pepper and 1/2 cup of the Parmesan in a large bowl and whisk to combine; set aside.

3. Heat the oil in a 10-inch cast iron or oven-safe nonstick skillet over medium heat until shimmering.

4. Add the artichokes in a single layer and cook, stirring occasionally, until lightly browned, 6 to 8 minutes.

5. Add the spinach and garlic, and toss until the spinach is wilted and almost all of the liquid is evaporated, about 2 minutes.

6. Spread everything into an even layer. Pour the egg mixture over the vegetables and sprinkle with the remaining 1/2 cup of Parmesan. Tilt the pan to make sure the eggs settle evenly over all the vegetables.

7. Cook undisturbed until the eggs at the edges of the pan begin to set, 2 to 3 minutes.

8. Bake until the eggs are completely set, 12 to 15 minutes. To check, cut a small slit in the center of the frittata. If raw eggs run into the cut, bake for another few minutes.

9. Cool in the pan for 5 minutes, then slice into wedges and serve warm.

MEAL 9: MEDITERRANEAN DIET

BREAKFAST PITA

Ingredients

- ✓ Four big eggs (must be at room temperature)

- ✓ Salt

- ✓ A pair of whole-wheat breads (pita) divided into equal parts of two.

- ✓ Half a cup of hummus, or four ounces.

- ✓ A piece of medium sized cucumber, sliced into thin rounds.

- ✓ A pair of medium size tomatoes diced into large portions.

- ✓ Freshly plucked, roughly chopped parsley leaves. A handful.

- ✓ Black Pepper, freshly ground.

- ✓ Hot sauce (optional)

Preparation

1. Get a medium sauce pan. Fill with water and boil. Gently put the eggs (still at room temperature) and let them cook for about seven minutes.

2. Drain the water, and let the eggs cool off under running water. Remove the egg shells and cut them into four quarter slices, inch thick.

3. Sprinkle salt on them and keep them aside.

4. Fill the inside of each pita pocket with 2 tablespoons of hummus. Take a few slices of cucumber as well as some pieces of diced tomatoes, put them in each pita.

5. Season with pepper and salt to taste.

6. Shove a slice of egg into each of the pitas and add a sprinkling of parsley and, if you want, hot sauce.

7. Serve.

MEAL 10: MUESLI

Ingredients

- ✓ Half a cup of wheat bran.

- ✓ Three half-filled cups of rolled oats.

- ✓ Half a teaspoon of kosher salt

- ✓ Half a teaspoon of ground cinnamon

- ✓ Half a cup of sliced almonds

- ✓ A quarter of a cup of raw pecans, chopped roughly.

- ✓ A quarter of a cup of raw pepitas (pumpkin seeds that have been shelled)

- ✓ A quarter of a cup of coconut flakes (unsweetened)

- ✓ A quarter of a cup of roughly chopped apricots (dried)

- ✓ A quarter of a cup of dried cherries.

Preparation

1. Toast the nuts, seeds and grains. Set up two racks to part the oven into three and heat up to 350°F.

2. Place the wheat bran, oats, cinnamon and salt, onto a baking sheet (rimmed), then toss to enable them mix well as well as spread into an equal layer.

3. On the other baking sheet (also rimmed), place the pecans, pepitas and almonds and toss again to mix and spread evenly.

4. Next, move both sheets into the oven, with the oats on the upper rack and the nuts on the lower. Bake until nuts become fragrant, for about ten to twelve minutes.

5. Throw in the coconut. Withdraw the baking sheet containing the nuts and set it aside to cool off.

6. Sprinkle some coconut atop the oats before returning them to the top rack. Bake till the coconut turns golden-brown, for about five more minutes. Withdraw from the oven and let it cool down for up to ten minutes.

7. Move the contents of the two baking sheets into a large bowl.

8. Pour in the cherries and apricots and toss to mix it up.

9. You'll need an airtight container to transfer the mixture to. Inside an airtight container, muesli can be stored for up to thirty days, at room temperature.

Use as you deem fit, as overnight oats, cereal, oatmeal or even with yogurt. You can top it with fresh fruits or drizzle maple syrup or honey over it if you wish.

PART TWO: LUNCH AND EVENING MEALS

MEAL 1: EGG NOODLES (WITH WALNUTS &

BASIL)

Ingredients

- ✓ A pound of dried egg noodles

- ✓ Four tablespoons of olive oil (extra virgin)

- ✓ A piece of grated onion

- ✓ A cup of white wine

- ✓ A piece of chopped clove garlic

- ✓ A pound of fresh cubed tomatoes

- ✓ A cup of chopped walnuts

- ✓ 2 tablespoons of freshly chopped Basil, or a teaspoon if it's the dried variety

- ✓ Pepper and salt as you fancy.

- ✓ A teaspoon of sugar.

- ✓ A teaspoon of tomato paste

Preparation

1. Sauté onions in 2 tablespoons oil for 5 minutes. For about five minutes, sauté the onions in two tablespoons of oil.

2. Next, add the tomatoes, garlic and wine. Allow to simmer for about fifteen minutes.

3. Pour in the Basil, salt, sugar, pepper, tomato paste and the walnuts.

4. Simmer until the mixture is thick. Should take around ten minutes.

5. The eggs noodles should be cooked according to the instructions labelled on the package. Add two tablespoons of oil after straining the noodles.

6. Then add your sauce and toss to mix it up.

7. You may serve with parmesan cheese, newly grated.

MEAL 2: LEEKS & CELERY

Ingredients

- ✓ Half a cup of olive oil (extra virgin)

- ✓ A pound of thin celery

- ✓ A pound of leeks (only the white parts) roundly and think cut.

- ✓ A large piece of chopped onion

- ✓ A cup of tomatoes (grated)

- ✓ One and half cups of water

- ✓ Pepper and salt to your individual taste.

- ✓ Nutmeg.

Preparation

1. Both leeks and celery should be sauté in oil (olive) for up to five minutes.

2. Add the tomatoes and onions to mix and sauté for another five minutes.

3. Next, add the recommended volume of water and allow to simmer for half an hour. Season to taste with salt and pepper.

4. Once the meal is done, add a very light sprinkling of nutmeg.

MEAL 3: HALIBUT WITH ROSEMARY

Ingredients

- ✓ Four halibut steaks (6-ounce each)

- ✓ Two pieces of onions, finely chopped

- ✓ A couple cloves of mashed garlic

- ✓ Half a cup of olive oil (extra virgin)

- ✓ Three small cubes of fresh tomatoes.

- ✓ Half a cup of lemon juice (fresh)

- ✓ Two tablespoons of either fresh or dried rosemary.

- ✓ Salt and pepper, as you deem necessary.

- ✓ A tbsp of mustard

Preparation

1. Preheat your oven to 350° F.

2. For five minutes, sauté the garlic and onions in extra virgin olive oil.

3. Add your mustard, salt and pepper seasoning, rosemary, lemon juice and tomatoes. Sauté for another five minutes.

4. Slightly oil a baking dish, then place the steaks on one of its layers. Cover it with the rosemary mixture.

5. Cover the baking dish carefully with foil and allow it bake for half an hour.

MEAL 4: CARROT, CUCUMBER & BEET SALAD

Ingredients

✓ One whole cucumber, sliced into perfect rounds.

✓ One grated carrot.

✓ 1 small or 1/2 large beet, grated One small or half of a large beet (grated)

THE MEDITERRANEAN DIET FOR BEGINNERS

✓ Dark green lettuce (a handful will do fine)

✓ A quarter of a cup of Dijon vinaigrette

Preparation

1. Add all vegetables into a salad bowl.

2. Toss with Dijon vinaigrette.

3. Serve.

MEAL 5: BEEF + HERBS & EGGPLANT

Ingredients

✓ Two pounds of lean beef, divided into bite-sized cubes

✓ Five tbsp of olive oil (extra virgin)

✓ Two chopped onions

✓ One lb of sliced zucchini

✓ One lb of cubed eggplant,

✓ A teaspoon of thyme (thyme)

✓ A teaspoon of sage (dried)

✓ Two tablespoons of chopped fresh mint

✓ Salt and pepper, as deemed necessary.

Preparation

1. Heat one half of the oil in a pot. Cook the meat till brown. Cover meat with water and allow to simmer.

2. Using another pot, pour in the other half of the oil and sauté the veggies and onions until they become soft. This should take about ten minutes.

3. Add the tomatoes and stir. Then join the veggies mixture with the meat.

4. Pour in the sage, mint and thyme. Add pepper and salt as your taste buds decide and bring to meal to a boil. Allow to simmer for forty-five minutes.

MEAL 6: STUFFED TOMATOES & PEPPERS

Ingredients

- ✓ Five pieces of tomatoes
- ✓ Five pieces of any of red or green peppers
- ✓ A cup of parsley with all the stems removed
- ✓ A cup of dill with all stems removed

- ✓ Two large pieces of onions, divided into quarters

- ✓ A cup of water

- ✓ A tablespoon of tomato paste

- ✓ One cup of uncooked rice

- ✓ Half a cup of olive oil (extra virgin)

- ✓ A teaspoon of salt

- ✓ Half a teaspoon of pepper

For the sauce:

- ✓ Half a cup of the extra virgin olive oil

- ✓ One tablespoon of tomato paste

- ✓ One cup of water

- ✓ Half a teaspoon salt

- ✓ Just a pinch of pepper

Preparation

1. Your oven should be preheated to 350° F.

2. See that the tomatoes are washed. Then slice the tops nearly off. Leave a tiny part hanging, creating a sort of "hinge."

3. Using a spoon, scoop the tomato's insides out, leaving the pulp to be used for stuffing.

4. In the same way, wash the peppers. Create the hinge effect by almost slicing the top off, just leaving a bit of it attached in the end. Remove the seeds and discard them.

5. Using a blender, mix the insides of the scooped tomatoes, the parsley, the onions, dills a cup of water, and of course, the tomato paste; blend together for up to 2 minutes.

6. After blending, transfer the mixture into a bowl. Add in the oil, rice, pepper, and salt, and mix properly with a spoon.

7. Next, fill each of the tomato/peppers with the vegetables and rice mixture and place it on a casserole dish.

8. To make the sauce, mix the half cup of olive oil, water, tomato paste, pepper, and salt. Then cover the peppers and tomatoes with the salt.

9. Then bake uncovered for an hour till the rice is cooked.

MEAL 7: BEANS (BLACK-EYED) WITH HERBS

Ingredients

- ✓ Half a cup of extra virgin olive oil.

- ✓ Two big cans or four small cans of black-eyed peas.

  (29oz/15oz)

- ✓ A cup of fresh chopped parsley, with the stems, removed

- ✓ 1 cup fresh dill, stems removed, chopped.

- ✓ Four green thinly sliced onions

- ✓ Two peeled and grated carrots

- ✓ Two bay leaves

- ✓ Two orange slices with flesh and peel.

- ✓ Salt and pepper, as your taste buds, deem necessary.

- ✓ Two tbsp of tomato paste.

Preparation

1. Drain the beans, reserve liquid.

2. Using a deep pot, heat the oil. Sauté parsley, onions, carrots, dill, and beans for about 3 minutes.

3. Add a cup of water, 2 cups of the liquid reserved from draining the beans, orange peel, bay leaves, and tomato paste.

4. Stir and allow to cook for half an hour.

5. Add salt and pepper to taste. Add pepper and salt as deemed necessary.

MEAL 8: CLASSIC MEDITERRANEAN SALAD

Ingredients

- ✓ One torn medium-romaine lettuce head

- ✓ Three small sized tomatoes, smoothly sliced

- ✓ One medium-sized cucumber, sliced into pieces

- ✓ Green bell pepper, small-sized and sliced

- ✓ A small piece of onion, sliced into little rings

- ✓ Six thinly sliced radishes,

- ✓ Chopped parsley,

- ✓ Three tablespoons of lemon juice

✓ Olive oil

✓ A clove of crushed garlic

✓ Pepper & salt to taste

✓ A tablespoon of mint

✓ Halved pieces of pita pocket bread

Preparation

1. Mix tomatoes, lettuce, onion, pepper, parsley, and radishes in a small salad bowl

2. Put the lemon juice, olive oil, green bell pepper, salt, garlic, and mint together and whisk thoroughly.

3. Spread the mixture over the salad and toss to make sure the coating is thorough.

4. Serve.

MEAL 9: SALMON AND COUSCOUS

CASSEROLE

Ingredients

- ✓ A cup of water

- ✓ Two cloves of minced garlic

- ✓ Two-thirds of a cup of couscous (whole wheat)

- ✓ Drain a can (14.75 ounces) of salmon. Ensure it is flaked and the bones and skins completely removed.

- ✓ Two cups of spinach baby leaves, fresh and packaged

- ✓ Half a cup of red sweet pepper. Must be jarred, roasted, well-drained, and chopped.

- ✓ One-third of a cup of Tomato Bruschetta topper (jarred)

- ✓ Two tablespoons of almonds (purchased and toasted)

Preparation

1. Put the garlic and water in a two-quart microwave with a safe-casserole.

2. Leave the microwave uncovered and the heat at 100% for two to three minutes, until the mixture begins to boil.

3. Extract mixture from the microwave, add to couscous, and stir.

4. Spoon some salmon on the mixture. Cover and let it be for five minutes.

5. Join the roasted peppers, bruschetta topper, and spinach to the couscous mixture. Toss to allow it mix well.

6. Pour the mix equally into four serving plates. Add almonds as toppings.

Tip: If toasted almonds aren't available, you can toast your almonds or use the untoasted variety. If you want to toast your own, your oven must be preheated to 350° F. In a single layer, spread the almonds in a pie pan and bake for up to 10 minutes or until you get that light brown color. Stir from time to time. Don't use it until it's completely cool.

MEAL 10: QUINOA-STUFFED EGGPLANT

WITH TAHINI SAUCE

Ingredients

- ✓ One eggplant

- ✓ Two tablespoons of divided olive oil

- ✓ A medium-sized piece of diced shallot (half a cup)

- ✓ A cup of chopped button mushrooms (two cups whole)

- ✓ Five to six pieces of plum Tuttorosso tomatoes (chopped)

- ✓ One tbsp of tomato juice scooped from the can.

- ✓ Two cloves of minced garlic

- ✓ 1/2 cup cooked quinoa Half a cup of quinoa (cooked)

- ✓ Half a tsp of ground cumin.

- ✓ One tbsp of fresh parsley, finely chopped. (Plus some more for garnish)

- ✓ Salt & pepper to taste pepper and salt to your taste

- ✓ One tbsp of tahini

- ✓ One tsp of lemon juice

- ✓ Half a tsp of garlic powder

✓ Water (to thin)

Preparation

1. Heat your oven to 425°F.

2. Divide the eggplant into two equal parts lengthwise and extract a little bit of the flesh. Get a baking sheet and place it on it, then drizzle with a tablespoon of olive oil.

3. Add a sprinkling of salt and bake for up to twenty minutes.

4. As the eggplant cooks in the oven, put the remaining oil in a big skillet and heat.

5. Next, add the mushrooms and shallot and sauté for about five minutes, until the mushrooms are soft.

6. Add the spices, quinoa, and tomatoes and let them cook until the liquid evaporates.

7. After cooking the eggplant for twenty minutes, lower the oven temperature to 350°F and fill each half with the quinoa-tomato mix. Let it bake for a further ten minutes.

8. Once you're ready to serve, whisk the lemon, tahini, water, garlic altogether, and add just a touch of pepper and salt. Then drizzle the tahini atop the eggplant with a sprinkling of parsley and enjoy your meal!

PART THREE: SALADS

Meal 1: Green Salad + Artichokes & Olives

Ingredients

- ✓ One romaine lettuce heart (six ounces), divided into inch pieces.

- ✓ Three ounces or three cups of baby arugula

- ✓ 1/3 cups of freshly cut parsley leaves.

- ✓ A cup of whole baby artichoke. Soaked in water, evenly quartered, then rinsed and dried.

- ✓ Two tablespoons of either white balsamic vinegar or white wine vinegar.

- ✓ 1/3 cup of pitted and halved kalamata olives.

- ✓ A small piece of minced garlic clove

- ✓ Pepper and salt

- ✓ Three tbsp of olive oil (Olive oil)

- ✓ One ounce of shaved Asiago cheese.

Preparation

1. Put the arugula, parsley, olives, artichoke hearts, and romaine in a large size bowl. Toss gently.

2. Put garlic, vinegar, a quarter of a teaspoon of salt, and a pinch of pepper together in one bowl and whisk.

3. As you constantly whisk, drizzle oil in slowly.

4. Also, drizzle your vinaigrette over the salad and toss gently to achieve even coating.

5. Add pepper and salt seasoning to your taste.

6. Now you can serve the meal, topping each individual's portions with the delicious Asiago.

Meal 2: Arugula Salad + Fennel & Shaved Parmesan

Ingredients

✓ A large bulb of fennel with the stalks discarded, and the bulb halved and sliced thin after it has been cored.

✓ Six ounces or six cups of baby arugula.

✓ One and a half tablespoons of lemon juice

✓ One small minced shallot.

✓ A teaspoon of fresh thyme (minced)

✓ A teaspoon of Dijon mustard.

✓ A small piece of minced garlic clove

✓ A quarter of olive oil (extra virgin)

✓ Pepper and salt.

✓ An ounce of shaved Parmesan cheese

Preparation

1. Place the fennel and arugula hearts together in a large bowl and toss gently.

2. Put garlic, thyme, mustard, lemon juice vinegar, shallot, a one-eighth of a teaspoon of salt, and a pinch of pepper together in one bowl and whisk.

3. As you consistently whisk, drizzle in the oil slowly.

4. Sprinkle some dressing over the salad and toss gently to aid coating.

5. Add salt and pepper to your own taste.

6. Serve the meal. You may top each person's plate with Parmesan.

MEAL 3: SALADE NIÇOISE

Ingredients

- ✓ Dressing

- ✓ Two lemons and a quarter of a cup of lemon juice.

- ✓ One minced shallot.

- ✓ Two teaspoons of freshly minced thyme.

- ✓ Two tablespoons of minced fresh Basil.

- ✓ Two teaspoons of fresh minced oregano

- ✓ A teaspoon of Dijon mustard

- ✓ Half a teaspoon of salt

- ✓ A quarter of a teaspoon of pepper

- ✓ Half a cup of extra-virgin olive oil

- ✓ Salad

- ✓ One one-quarter pound of small red unpeeled potatoes (quartered)

- ✓ Salt and pepper

✓ Two tablespoons of vermouth (dry)

✓ Two heads of Bibb or Boston lettuce (just a pound), tear it into bite-size pieces

✓ Two (five-ounce) cans of solid white tuna in water. Drained and flaked tuna precisely.

✓ Three smaller sized tomatoes cored diced into pieces.

✓ Wedges (half-inch-thick)

✓ A small piece of red onion, thinly sliced

✓ Eight ounces of green beans, carefully trimmed and then halved.

✓ Three peeled hard-cooked large eggs, quartered

✓ A quarter of a cup of pitted (niçoise) olives

✓ Ten to twelve rinsed anchovy fillets

✓ Two tablespoons of rinsed capers

Preparation

The Dressing

1. Put lemon juice, Basil, mustard, shallot, oregano, thyme, salt, and pepper all in a tiny bowl. Whisk continuously.

2. As you whisk, gently drizzle in the oil.

For the Salad

1. Find a spacious saucepan. Pour the potatoes in the saucepan and pour in enough water to cover up to an inch. Then boil on high heat.

2. Add a tablespoon of salt and reduce the heat to allow it to simmer. Cook till potatoes are tender enough to take in a paring knife without much effort. It should take about five to eight minutes.

3. Using a slotted spoon, gently remove the potatoes into a bowl, without discarding the water.

4. Add a quarter of a cup of vermouth and vinaigrette to the warm potatoes, then toss.

5. Add salt and pepper as you deem necessary.

6. As the potatoes cook, put lettuce in a bowl and add a quarter of a vinaigrette cup. Toss until it's evenly coated.

7. Get a very big and flat serving platter and carefully place a bed of lettuce on it.

8. Put the tuna in the bowl, now empty. Using a fork, break it up.

9. Add a quarter of a cup of the vinaigrette and combine by stirring.

10. Right in the center of the lettuce, mound the tuna.

11. As the bowl is now empty, take tomatoes, red onions, and two tablespoons of vinaigrette, salt, and pepper and place them all in the bowl. Then toss to aid coating.

12. In mounds around the corners of the lettuce bed, place the onion-tomato mix.

13. Reserved potatoes should be arranged separately in other mounds at the edge of the bed.

14. Boil water and add a tablespoon of both salt and green beans.

15. Cook till it gets crispy and tender. It should take three to five minutes.

16. While you do this, fill a large bowl to I middle with ice and water.

17. Drain the beans, move to the ice water. Let it cool for about thirty seconds.

18. Move the beans to a three-layered paper towel and ensure it is properly dried.

19. The bowl is now empty so pour the green beans and the remaining two spoons of vinaigrette. Season to your taste with salt and pepper, then toss.

20. Arrange in yet other different mounds at the corners of the lettuce bed.

21. In separate mounds, arrange olives, eggs, and anchovies at the corners of the lettuce bed.

22. Sprinkle entire salad with capers, if using. Add a generous sprinkling of capers to the entire salad.

23. Ready to serve.

MEAL 4: WARM SPINACH SALAD WITH FETA

& PISTACHIOS

Ingredients

- ✓ One and a half ounces (or ⅓) of crumbled feta cheese

- ✓ Three tablespoons of (extra-virgin) olive oil

- ✓ A two-inch strip of lemon zest.

- ✓ One and a half tablespoons of juice

- ✓ One minced shallot,

- ✓ Two teaspoons of sugar

- ✓ Ten ounces of spinach (curly leaf type) stemmed and pieces into bite-size.

- ✓ Six trimmed and sliced thin radishes

- ✓ Three tablespoons of chopped & toasted pistachios

- ✓ Salt and pepper to taste

Preparation

1. Put the Fetta on a plate. Let it freeze till it looks slightly firm, for about 15 minutes.

2. Cook the lemon zest, oil, sugar, and shallot in a Dutch oven over either low or medium heat, till shallot is considerably softened. This should take about five minutes.

3. Next, turn off the heat, remove the zest, add lemon juice, and stir. Then put the spinach and cover the lid and let it the steam heat till it's about to wilt. It shouldn't take more than thirty seconds.

4. Transfer spinach mixture and liquid left in the pot to a large bowl. Add radishes, pistachios, and chilled feta and toss to combine—season with salt and pepper to taste.

5. Move the spinach mix and the remnants of the liquid in the pot to a spacious bowl.

6. Put the pistachios, chilled Fetta and radishes, then toss to allow it mix well. Add salt and pepper to your taste.

7. Serve.

MEAL 5: ASPARAGUS SALAD WITH FETA, HAZELNUTS & ORANGES

Ingredients

Pesto

- ✓ Two cups of mint leaves (fresh)

- ✓ A quarter of a cup of fresh basil leaves

- ✓ A quarter of a cup of grated Pecorino Romano cheese

- ✓ A teaspoon of well-grated lemon zest

- ✓ Two teaspoons of juice

- ✓ A piece of minced garlic clove,

- ✓ Salt and pepper

- ✓ Half a cup of extra-virgin olive oil

Salad

- ✓ Two pounds of trimmed asparagus

- ✓ Two oranges

- ✓ Four ounces (a cup) of crumbled fetta cheese,

✓ Three-quarters cup of skinned, toasted, and chopped

hazelnuts

✓ Salt and pepper

Preparation

For the Pesto

1. You'll need a food processor. Take the Basil, mint, garlic, lemon juice and zest, pecorino, and three-quarters of a salt teaspoon. Pour everything in the food processor and for about twenty seconds.

2. Move the mixture to a large bowl. Add oil and stir with pepper and salt to taste.

For the Salad

1. Cut the tips of asparagus from the stalks into about pieces three-quarters inch long.

2. Slice the stalks one-eighth inch thick into approximate pieces of two inches long.

3. Remove the pitch and peel from the oranges.

4. Use a paring knife to release segments by slicing between membranes while holding the fruit atop the bowl.

5. Add the tips and stalks from the asparagus, the segments from the oranges, hazelnuts, and Fetta to the pesto. Then toss to mix well.

6. Season with pepper and salt to your own taste.

7. Serve meal.

MEAL 6: GREEN BEAN SALAD + CILANTRO SAUCE

Ingredients

- ✓ A quarter cup of walnuts
- ✓ 2 pieces of unpeeled garlic cloves
- ✓ Two and a half cups of fresh cilantro leaf and stems. All tough stem ends should be trimmed (about 2 bunches)
- ✓ Half a cup of (extra-virgin) olive oil
- ✓ Four teaspoons of lemon juice
- ✓ One sliced thin scallion

✓ Pepper and salt

✓ 2 pounds of trimmed green beans

Preparation

1. Over medium heat, cook the walnuts and garlic. Use an eight-inch skillet. Stir consistently until it turns toasted and fragrant—about five to seven minutes tops.

2. Move to a bowl and let the garlic cool for a bit. Then chop coarsely.

3. Using a food processor, process the likes of garlic, walnuts, lemon juice, oil, cilantro, salt (half a teaspoon), and pepper (⅛ teaspoon) for about sixty seconds. You might want to scrape down the sides if you wish, before moving to another bowl.

4. Add four quarts of water to a large pot and let it boil over high heat.

5. Fill a big bowl to the midpoint with ice and water.

6. Put a tablespoon of salt and green beans in the boiling water and cook for three to five minutes till it's crispy and tender.

7. Remove the green beans from the water, drain and move to the iced water. Let it cool for a couple of minutes.

8. Move the green beans to the bowl that contains the cilantro sauce and toss gently until everything is equally coated.

9. Season your salad with salt and pepper to your taste.

10. Serve or refrigerate.

Note that this salad can be kept in a refrigerator for only up to four hours.

MEAL 7: WALNUT, SPINACH & FETTA PASTA

SALAD

Ingredients

- ✓ Two hundred and fifty grams of your best pasta

- ✓ Two hundred and fifty grams of Fetta. (Lemnos Persian Marinated)

- ✓ A cup of walnuts, toasted and chopped

- ✓ A punnet of cherry tomatoes, divided into half

- ✓ Hundred grams of freshly washed baby spinach

- ✓ Four medium pieces of finely sliced shallots.

- ✓ Some parsley leaves for aesthetics.

The Dressing

- ✓ Three tablespoons of walnut oil (or extra virgin olive oil)

- ✓ Three tablespoons of red wine vinegar

- ✓ One medium clove of crushed garlic

- ✓ A teaspoon of Dijon mustard

- ✓ Newly ground black pepper and sea salt.

Preparation

1. Like the instructions on the packet says, cook your pasta to barely 'al dente.' Sieve the pasta of water and add a bit of olive oil or walnut. Set it aside.

2. Drain the Fetta too.

3. Remove the herbs and all peppercorns. Break the fetta pieces slightly, but keep some of the oil.

4. Use a large serving bowl for the dressing. Mix the oil, garlic, mustard, and vinegar; add pepper and salt to your taste.

5. Take a tablespoon of oil from the can, with the tomatoes, spinach, walnuts, and marinated Fetta.

6. Add to the dressing. Throw the pasta in the mix and taste for seasoning. Scatter parsley leaves on it.

7. Cover the lid and refrigerate for later, or begin to serve immediately.

MEAL 8: WATERMELON, QUINOA SALAD &

HALLOUMI

Ingredients

- ✓ Five hundred grams of seedless watermelon, cut into a baton shape

- ✓ One hundred and eighty grams of Lemnos Haloumi, cut into batons shape

- ✓ One and a half cups of cooked white quinoa

- ✓ Fifty grams of washed baby spinach leaves

- ✓ Fifty grams of toasted pine nuts

- ✓ Half a cup each of both parsley and mint leaves.

- ✓ Half a piece of finely sliced medium red onion

- ✓ Three tablespoons of olive oil

- ✓ Zest & juice of 1 lemon

- ✓ Newly ground black pepper & sea salt

Preparation

1. Use a large-sized frying pan and medium heat. Add the Lemnos Haloumi and one tablespoon of olive oil.

2. Fry each side for a minute or two, or till it turns golden. Set aside for a bit.

3. Take a large bowl and add the already cooked quinoa to it, alongside the spinach, herbs, juice and lemon zest, olive oil, and the watermelon batons. Toss everything well and add seasoning to your preferred taste.

4. Transfer to a platter, top with the toasted halloumi.

5. Serve.

MEAL 9: MIXED TOMATO SALAD +

TOASTED HALOUMI

Ingredients

- ✓ One 180g pack of Lemnos Haloumi

- ✓ One sliced Punnet Heirloom tomatoes

- ✓ Two really ripe and large sliced tomatoes

- ✓ One peeled and thinly sliced small red onion

- ✓ Olive oil to drizzle (extra virgin)

- ✓ Basil leaves

- ✓ Newly ground black pepper & sea salt

- ✓ Dukkha (not compulsory)

Preparation

1. Brush a flat barbecue plate or spacious frying pan with a bit of Olive oil.

2. Divide the Haloumi into slim wedges, then fry gently on medium heat till it turns a good golden brown.

3. Pile the sliced tomatoes, red onion, and toasted Haloumi on the serving plate.

4. Season with some salt and black pepper and then round up the meal by drizzling some olive oil (extra virgin) and a scattering of fresh basil leaves. If you're using Dukkha, this is the time to add it.

MEAL 10: QUINOA & HALOUMI SALAD + CHILLI CORIANDER DRESSING

Ingredients

- ✓ One large peeled, thickly sliced kumara (orange sweet potato) halved lengthways

- ✓ One red onion, cut into wedges

- ✓ One teaspoon of cumin seeds

- ✓ Half a teaspoon of ground coriander

- ✓ A quarter of a cup of olive oil (60ml)

- ✓ Two cups of fresh vegetable stock (500ml)

- ✓ A cup of rinsed and drained quinoa (200g)

Preparation

1. Preheat your oven to 200°C. Line one baking tray with sufficient baking paper.

2. Combine the onion, kumara, cumin, the ground coriander, and 1 tablespoon of oil in one large bowl.

3. Season with salt and pepper to your taste. Arrange the mixture in a single layer over the lined tray.

4. Now roast, turning it from time to time, for about twenty minutes or until it turns golden brown and tender. Set aside to cool considerably.

5. While you do that, mix the quinoa and stock in a big saucepan over high-level heat. Reduce the heat when it boils. Then simmer and cover the lid for about ten minutes or until it becomes tender.

6. Turn off the heat and cover the lid for about ten minutes.

7. Chop a quarter of the coriander finely. Then place it in a jar with a screw top, alongside the lemon juice, the chili,

and half of the oil left. Shake till it mixes properly and add salt and pepper to your taste.

8. Heat what's left of the oil in a big frying pan on high heat.

9. Cook the halloumi for a minute or two on each side or till it turns golden brown. Then move it to a plate.

10. Put the quinoa, kumara mixture, and the rest of the coriander in the big bowl. Align them on a serving platter and top with the Haloumi and a drizzling of coriander dressing.

11. Serve instantly with a sprinkling of lemon zest.

PART THREE:

MEDITERRANEAN

APPETIZERS

MEAL 1: CARAMELIZED ONION, HALOUMI

& CHICKPEA FRITTERS

Ingredients

- ✓ One hundred and eighty grams of coarsely grated Lemnos Haloumi

- ✓ Four Hundred grams can of drained chickpeas

- ✓ Two medium-sized and finely sliced brown onions

- ✓ Half a cup of either chickpea or besan flour

- ✓ A tablespoon of turmeric powder

- ✓ A tablespoon of smoked sweet paprika

- ✓ Two tablespoons of curry powder

- ✓ Two tablespoons of olive oil

- ✓ Two lightly beaten eggs

- ✓ Sea salt & newly ground black pepper

- ✓ Dipping sauce (not compulsory)

- ✓ Hundred grams of Lemnos Smooth Fetta

- ✓ A cup of plain Greek-style yogurt

- ✓ A piece of crushed medium clove garlic

 ✓ 2 tablespoons of chopped fresh mint

Preparation

1. Heat a large-sized frying pan over medium heat.

2. Add a tablespoon of olive oil and your onions. Fry for up to ten minutes, stirring from time to time until the onion begins to soften and caramelizes, turning a dark brown color.

3. Add the spices and curry powder. Cook for a further thirty seconds, stirring consistently or until the spices begin to smell wonderful. Turn off the heat and let the onion mix cool a little.

4. Add the drained chickpeas, grated Haloumi, chickpea flour, cooled mix of onions and spice, and the eggs into a large bowl before stirring comprehensively.

5. Add seasoning to your taste.

6. Using medium heat, pour the oil left in a frying pan with a heavy bottom.

7. Heap teaspoons of the Haloumi and chickpeas mix and fry until both sides turn a golden-brown color.

8. Drain with kitchen paper.

9. Put all the sauce condiments in a food processor and process until everything is smooth.

10. Your warm Haloumi fritters are ready to serve with dipping sauce if you wish.

MEAL 2: ROASTED BEETROOT & FETTA DIP

+ RAW VEGETABLES

Ingredients

- ✓ Two hundred grams of Lemnos Smooth Fetta, shattered into pieces
- ✓ Two medium-sized beetroot
- ✓ Two hundred milligrams of pot crème Fraiche
- ✓ Two tablespoons of freshly chopped dill
- ✓ Two crushed pieces of medium-sized cloves of garlic.
- ✓ One tablespoon of lemon juice

✓ Sea salt & pepper

✓ Two peeled carrots, cut into a baton-like shape

✓ One Lebanese cucumber, cut into baton-like shape.

✓ Half of the red capsicum, cut into a baton-like shape.

✓ One small bunch of washed and trimmed radishes.

Preparation

1. Preheat your oven to 180°.

2. Wash the beetroot and trim it. Wrap firmly in foil and bake for about thirty-five to forty minutes or until it turns tender, checked with a knife or skewer.

3. Let the beetroot cool, still wrapped in foil. Then take off the foil, remove all stalks, and peel off the skin.

4. In a food processor, add the Lemnos Smooth Fetta, peeled cooked beetroot, dill, crème Fraiche, crushed garlic, and blitz until smooth. Season to taste with lemon juice, salt, and pepper.

5. Add the Fetta, peeled beetroot, crème Fraiche, dill and process until it's smooth enough. Season to your personal taste with salt, pepper, and lemon juice.

6. Move the dip to another bowl and serve with crispy veggies for smooth dipping.

MEAL 3: SPICY BAKED FETTA WITH TOMATOES

Ingredients

- ✓ One hundred and eighty grams of Lemnos Traditional Fetta halved.
- ✓ One large finely diced ripe tomato
- ✓ Either of a large shallot or a small red onion cut into fine slices
- ✓ One long red chili, finely sliced
- ✓ Two tablespoons of olive oil (extra virgin)
- ✓ A tablespoon of oregano (dried)

Preparation

1. Preheat your oven to 180°.

2. Mix the chili, diced onions, and tomato together.

3. Using two large sheets of baking paper, place the Fetta in the middle of each sheet. Then top each sheet with a piece of Fetta and half of the tomato and chili mixture.

4. Next, drizzle with olive oil (extra virgin) and sprinkle thoroughly with dried oregano.

5. Pick up all edges of the baking paper and fold together to make tight parcels. Move both parcels to an ovenproof dish that is the right fit for them.

6. Proceed to bake in an oven until both of the vegetables and Fetta have softened considerably, do this for about twenty minutes.

7. Unwrap the parcels and proceed to serve the hot baked Fetta alongside crusty bread to serve as dipping.

MEAL 4: WHITE BEAN AND FETTA DIP +

HOMEMADE PITTA CHIPS

Ingredients

- ✓ Two hundred grams of Fetta broken into pieces

- ✓ Four hundred grams of drained canned cannellini beans

- ✓ Two medium cloves of crushed garlic

- ✓ One tablespoon of lemon juice

- ✓ Salt and newly ground pepper to your taste

- ✓ Pitta chips

- ✓ Three medium loaves of pitta bread

- ✓ Two tablespoons of olive oil (extra virgin)

- ✓ Two teaspoons of smoked sweet paprika

- ✓ A tablespoon of sesame seeds

- ✓ Sea salt

Preparation

1. Preheat your oven to 170°.

2. Add to each pitta bread a little olive oil scattered lightly with sesame seeds, sea salt, and paprika's faint dusting.

3. Slice the bread into several long wedges each and move in one layer to two big oven trays.

4. Then bake in the already heated oven for about ten minutes or until it turns golden crisp.

5. Add the Fetta, crushed garlic, and drained cannellini beans and process until you get that smooth blend. Season with salt, pepper, and lemon juice.

6. Your Fetta and bean dip is ready to serve right away with warm pitta chips.

MEAL 5: ROASTED CAPSICUM DIP WITH TOASTED PIDE BREAD

Ingredients

- ✓ Two large red capsicums

- ✓ Two hundred gram of Fetta

- ✓ Half of a finely diced red onion

- ✓ Two tablespoons of chopped fresh dill

- ✓ Two tablespoons of olive oil

- ✓ Two tablespoons of fresh lemon

- ✓ Sea salt and freshly ground black pepper

- ✓ Two flat pied bread, or any other flatbread.

- ✓ One teaspoon of smoked sweet paprika

- ✓ Some dill fronds for aesthetic purposes

Preparation

1. Preheat your oven to 180°.

2. Put the entire capsicums on a baking tray and drizzle a bit of olive oil on it.

3. Cook for some thirty to thirty-five minutes, or until the skin starts to blacken and the capsicums begin to soften or collapse.

4. Transfer it from the oven and wrap it very tightly with foil. Let it cool to make it easier for the skin to slip off.

5. Once it cools, peel off the skin and extract the seeds. Place the capsicums in a food processor.

6. Break off a tiny piece of Fetta from the block (you can crumble it over the dipping sauce much later).

7. Pour the remaining Fetta and capsicums, onion, dill, salt, and pepper into a food processor and blend till you get that smoothness.

8. Move the mixture onto a serving dish and crumble the specially reserved Fetta over the top of the serving and some dill fronds.

9. The flatbread needs to be first cut into triangle shapes, then sprinkled with paprika with a light drizzling of olive oil.

10. Then put in back on the baking tray and in the oven. To bake till it turns crisp, you'll need about ten minutes.

11. Take the tray out of the oven and serve immediately with the dip before it gets cold.

MEAL 6: BATATA HARRA

Ingredients

- ✓ Four pieces of potatoes

- ✓ Three or four tablespoons of whichever kind of oil you prefer

- ✓ Three tablespoons of minced garlic

- ✓ Half a cup of minced cilantro

- ✓ One and three-quarters tablespoons of paprika

- ✓ A tsp of cayenne (Not compulsory)

- ✓ Salt to your preferred taste

- ✓ Two tablespoons of freshly extracted lemon juice

- ✓ Two tablespoons of minced parsley (quite tasty, but also not compulsory)

Preparation

1. Cube the potatoes, with or without the peel. Place in a safe microwave dish and add a tbsp of oil. Using a plastic wrap, cover tightly and leave in the microwave for about five to seven minutes.

2. Set your heat to medium-low and heat a pan containing two tablespoons of oil. Add some garlic and cover the lid. Cook for about three minutes, but try not to let the garlic burn.

3. Next, add the cilantro and let it wilt for a minute or two. Extract the sauce from the pan and put it aside.

4. Put a tablespoon of oil in a pan and heat over medium heat (it is advisable to use a non-stick pan to make your cleanup easier).

5. Next, add the potatoes but don't stir. Cook for a few minutes till they turn brown before turning each side with a spatula.

6. Cook until all sides are evenly browned.

7. Once the potatoes are cooked, take out into the dish. Add the cilantro-garlic sauce, lemon juice, paprika, cayenne (if using), and salt and toss.

8. As soon as the potatoes are well cooked, put in a dish, add your garlic-cilantro sauce, paprika, lemon juice, and cayenne (if used).

9. Then add salt and toss.

10. Serve.

MEAL 7: ROASTED RED PEPPER AND

ARTICHOKE TAPENADE

Ingredients

- ✓ A seven-ounce jar of red peppers, roasted, well-drained, and roughly chopped.

- ✓ A fourteen ounce can of well-drained and roughly chopped artichoke hearts.

- ✓ A third of a cup of fresh parsley, with the stems, removed.

- ✓ Half a cup of freshly grated Parmesan cheese.

- ✓ Three tablespoons of olive oil (extra virgin)

- ✓ A quarter of a cup of drained capers.

- ✓ Two cloves of minced garlic

- ✓ One or one and a half tablespoons of freshly made lemon juice

- ✓ For serving, a sixteen-ounce baguette loaf.

Preparation

1. Pour the roasted and drained red peppers and the artichoke hearts into a blend or food processor bowl.

2. Add fresh parsley, capers, lemon juice, garlic, parmesan cheese, and just a bit of olive oil.

3. Then, gently pulse until all ingredients are smoothly chopped, but not pureed completely.

4. Season, if you want, with pepper and salt to your taste and stir.

5. Serve with vegetable sticks and toasted slices of baguette loaf.

MEAL 8: ITALIAN ROASTED MUSHROOMS

AND VEGGIES

Ingredients

- ✓ An Lb of cleaned cremini mushrooms.
- ✓ Two cups of cauliflower chopped into tiny florets
- ✓ Two cups of cocktail tomatoes
- ✓ Twelve cloves of peeled garlic
- ✓ Two tablespoons of olive oil
- ✓ One tablespoon of Italian seasoning
- ✓ Salt and pepper to preferred taste.
- ✓ One tablespoon of fresh, chopped parsley

Preparation

1. Preheat your oven to a temperature of 400° F
2. Mix all veggies and mushrooms in a bowl, add a drizzle of olive oil, salt, pepper, Italian seasoning, and properly toss till it is well combined.

3. Pour the veggies in a baking sheet and put inside the preheated oven.

4. Roast for about twenty minutes to half an hour, until the mushrooms turn golden brown color and the cauliflowers are tender.

5. Before serving, add fresh parsley as garnish.

Suppose you have no Italian seasoning, no problem. You can as well use the same measured amount of rosemary, thyme, oregano, and basil.

MEAL 9: SKINNY GREEK LAYERED DIP

Ingredients

- ✓ Six inches of two whole wheat bread (pocket).

- ✓ Cooking spray

- ✓ A container of plain hummus (seven or eight Oz)

- ✓ A container of no-fat plain Greek yogurt (six Oz)

- ✓ A tbsp of chopped fresh parsley

- ✓ A tsp of freshly made lemon juice

✓ One-eighth of a tsp of pepper

✓ A medium-sized plum, seeded, and chopped (Roma).

✓ One-third of a cup of quartered and pitted kalamata olives

✓ One-third of a cup of well-chopped cucumber.

✓ Half of a cup of crumbled feta cheese (2 oz).

✓ A quarter of a cup of chopped four medium-sized green onions.

✓ A tsp of olive oil

✓ Half of a medium-sized cucumber (sliced)

✓ A medium red or green bell pepper well partitioned into strips.

Preparation

1. Heat your oven to a temperature of about 350°F. Horizontally, split each of the pitas bread, this will make two rounds.

2. Divide each round into wedges of six. Line them up on a big cookie sheet with a rough, ungreased surface. For about five seconds, spray cooking spray.

3. Bake for about ten minutes, till it becomes crisp and of a golden-brown color. Then let it cool.

4. As that goes on, spread the hummus either in a pie plate or on a shallow serving platter.

5. Also, in a little bowl, make a mixture of the parsley, yogurt, pepper, and lemon juice, then pour it over the hummus.

6. For toppings, add onions, fetta cheese, olives, chopped cucumber, and tomatoes. Then drizzle with olive oil.

7. Serve.

MEAL 10: MINI PIZZA APPETIZERS

Ingredients

- ✓ A short crust pastry.

- ✓ One clove of finely chopped onion

- ✓ A can of mushroom

- ✓ Four hundred grams of pulp tomato

- ✓ salt (to preferred taste)

- ✓ black pepper to preferred taste (ground)

✓ A can of anchovies

✓ Grated mozzarella cheese

Preparation

1. Preheat the oven to a temperature of 410°F.

2. Bring out the dough, and with either a glass or a pastry cutter, shape out circles 6cm in diameter.

3. Line them up on a baking tray.

4. Heat some of the Olive oil on low heat in a saucepan. Then cook the mushrooms, onions, pepper, salt, and tomato pulp.

5. With one tsp of the tomato mixture, garnish the tarts.

6. Add one piece of anchovy and a sprinkling of mozzarella.

7. For twenty minutes, bake the pizza.

PART FOUR: MAINS

MEAL 1: ROAST CARROT SOUP + FETTA

CRUMBLE

Ingredients

- ✓ One Hundred grams of Fetta crumbled into several pieces

- ✓ A kilogram of peeled and unevenly chopped carrots

- ✓ Three tablespoons of olive oil

- ✓ Two peeled and chopped large onions

- ✓ Two teaspoons of ground cumin

- ✓ Half a teaspoon of ground cinnamon

- ✓ One teaspoon of ground ginger

- ✓ Four cups of a low salt vegetable stock (One liter)

- ✓ A cup of water

- ✓ Sea salt & black pepper, freshly ground

Preparation

1. Preheat your oven to 180°.

2. Put all the carrots in the bowl and add a tablespoon of olive oil. Move contents to an oven tray and bake for

about thirty minutes until it becomes tender or turns golden.

3. Using a large pan over medium heat, add the rest of the Olive oil and chopped onions. Stir constantly while you sauté for five or six minutes.

4. Pour in the spices and let them fry for up to thirty seconds or till the pot turns fragrant.

5. Throw in the water, stock, and roast carrots. Cook for twenty minutes until the carrots soften up.

6. Season to taste. Blend together with a blender or food processor till you get that fine smooth mix. Add seasoning to your taste.

7. Serve your carrot soup hot, with a generous scattering of Fetta.

MEAL 2: EGGPLANT AND HALOUMI

BURGERS

Ingredients

- ✓ Three tablespoons of olive oil
- ✓ One eggplant, slice them into four round pieces at about two centimeters thick each.
- ✓ Two 180 grams pack of Haloumi
- ✓ Half a cup of good tomato relish
- ✓ A large ripe tomato, sliced into pieces.
- ✓ Twenty grams of a washed rocket or salad leaves
- ✓ Four loaves of bread rolls cut in equal halves and toasted.

Preparation

1. Cut the Haloumi in the middle, then take each half and further cut them into two thick pieces. You'll have four slices of flat cheese that way.

2. Fry the eggplant and oil in a large frying pan and on medium heat. Fry each side for a couple of minutes each and turn when it becomes tender and golden.

3. To keep it warm, take out the eggplant and wrap tightly with aluminum foil.

4. Using the same frying pan, fry the Haloumi pieces on either side till they turn a golden-brown color mix. Like the eggplant, keep them warm too.

5. Whenever you're ready to arrange the burgers, sprinkle the bottom of each bread with relish, add toppings of eggplant slices, rocket leaves, 2 Haloumi slices, and a few tomatoes slices.

6. Serve instantly.

MEAL 3: BAKED PUMPKIN & FETTA PASTA

Ingredients

- ✓ Four hundred grams of the pasta you enjoy most

- ✓ Six hundred grams of either butternut or peeled Kent pumpkin, cut into cubes of 2cm each.

- ✓ Two hundred and fifty grams of Fetta

- ✓ Three medium-sized cloves of chopped garlic

- ✓ Two medium-sized red onions cut into wedges

- ✓ Half a cup of vegetable stock

Preparation

1. The oven should be preheated to 180°.

2. Put all the cubes of pumpkin inside a bowl and add 2 tbsp of olive oil. Move to a big oven tray and bake till it starts to turn golden.

3. Using the manufacturer's manual, cook the pasta in a large pan. Use Al dente ⅔ of the time.

4. Drain the Fetta and take out the herbs and peppercorns.

5. Heat a sauté pan or frying pan on medium heat and toss in the remaining wedges of red onions and olive oil. Stir constantly as you sauté for six or seven minutes until the red onions begin to change color or soften.

6. Toss in the garlic—Cook for a further 60 seconds.

7. Add the spinach leaves and cook until they wilt.

8. Add both the Olive oil and the pumpkin it was used to cook. Move the mix to the other pan containing the pasta.

9. Pour in the drained Fetta, cream, ⅔ of the Parmesan, and stock inside the pan. Add season to your taste and stir.

10. Move the pumpkin, Fetta, and pasta to a big ovenproof dish. Sprinkle the remaining Parmesan on it and let it bake in the oven you preheated for half an hour. Look out for the golden color on time.

MEAL 4: ZUCCHINI STUFFED WITH

HALOUMI & FRESH HERBS

Ingredients

- ✓ Four large zucchinis

- ✓ 2 cups of cooked couscous

- ✓ 180 grams of grated Haloumi

- ✓ Zest of 1 piece of lemon

- ✓ Half a medium of finely diced red onion

- ✓ Half a cup of parsley, finely chopped

- ✓ Half a cup of basil leaves, finely chopped (leave aside some whole leaves to use as garnish)

- ✓ Half a cup oregano leaves, finely chopped.

- ✓ One bottle of tomato passata (700ml)

- ✓ Two cans of crushed tomatoes (400g)

- ✓ Sea salt & freshly ground black pepper

Preparation

1. Preheat your oven to about 180°.

2. Cut all the zucchini into halves and take out the inside with either a teaspoon or a melon baller. Be sure to leave a shell as thick as one centimeter. Next, dice the Zucchinis gotten from the insides.

3. The cooked couscous should be joined with half of the Haloumi (grated), lemon zest, herbs, onions, and diced zucchini. Add seasoning to your taste and put the achieved mixture into the empty zucchinis.

4. Pour both the tomatoes and the passata inside a baking dish, large and deep enough to hold everything.

5. Season properly and arrange the zucchinis on top. The tomato mix should reach about midpoint to the zucchinis.

6. Scatter the other 19 Haloumi on top of the zucchinis and cover with foil.

7. Bake the zucchinis in the oven for thirty to thirty-five minutes, until you can pierce through the zucchinis.

8. Take off the foil and put the dish back in the oven. Take it out when the cheese begins to turn golden brown.

9. Serve your zucchini with the tomato sauce it was baked in. Add a salad on top and few basil leaves for garnish.

MEAL 5: CHICKEN SHAWARMA

Ingredients

For the Chicken

- ✓ Half a cup of olive oil (extra virgin)

- ✓ Juice extracted from 1 lemon

- ✓ Three cloves of minced garlic

- ✓ Two tablespoons of kosher salt

- ✓ A teaspoon of ground cumin

- ✓ A teaspoon of ground coriander

- ✓ Half a teaspoon of black pepper (freshly ground)

- ✓ Half a teaspoon of ground turmeric

- ✓ A quarter teaspoon of ground cinnamon

- ✓ Half a teaspoon of cayenne pepper

- ✓ Two lb. of chicken thighs (boneless, skinless)

- ✓ Cooking spray

- ✓ One big onion, thinly sliced

For Yogurt Sauce

- ✓ Half a cup of Greek yogurt

- ✓ Juice of half a lemon

- ✓ A tablespoon of olive oil (extra virgin)

- ✓ Two cloves of smashed and minced garlic

- ✓ Kosher salt

- ✓ A pinch of red pepper flakes (crushed)

For Serving

- ✓ Warmed Pitas

- ✓ Romaine (chopped)

- ✓ Halved cherry tomatoes

- ✓ Thinly sliced cucumber

Preparation

1. Take a large bowl, whisk lemon juice, oil, seasoning, and garlic. Add your chicken and toss to spread the coat. Cover the lid and put in the refrigerator for about 2 hours at least, or overnight at most.

2. Preheat the oven to about 425°. Next, grease a huge baking sheet with sufficient measure of cooking spray.

3. Add your onions to the marinade and toss to spread the coat evenly. Take out both chicken and onion from the marinade and arrange them on the said baking sheet.

4. Now, bake until the chicken turns golden and thoroughly cooked for about half an hour. Let the chicken rest on your cutting board for 5 minutes to cool slightly, then begin to slice thinly.

5. While you do that, make your yogurt sauce: using a small bowl, whisk together lemon juice, yogurt, oil, and garlic.

6. Season with the recommended amount of salt and a nice pinch of red pepper flakes.

7. If you want to serve as the pita, top with onion, tomatoes, romaine, chicken, and yogurt sauce.

MEAL 6: MOROCCAN VEGETABLE TAGINE

Ingredients

- ✓ A quarter of a cup of extra virgin olive oil
- ✓ 2 peeled and chopped medium-sized yellow onions
- ✓ Eight–ten cloves of peeled and chopped garlic
- ✓ Two large peeled and chopped carrots,
- ✓ Two pieces of large russet potatoes, finely peeled and cubed
- ✓ A large sweet potato, well peeled and cubed
- ✓ Salt
- ✓ A tablespoon of Harissa spice blend
- ✓ A tablespoon of ground coriander
- ✓ A teaspoon of ground cinnamon
- ✓ Half teaspoon of ground turmeric
- ✓ Two cups of canned tomatoes (whole peeled)
- ✓ Half a cup of heaping chopped dried apricot

- ✓ One quart of low-sodium vegetable broth (or broth of your choice)

- ✓ Two cups of cooked chickpeas

- ✓ One lemon, juice of

- ✓ A handful of fresh parsley leaves

Preparation

1. Heat the Olive oil and onions in a Dutch oven or heavy pot using medium-high heat. Sauté carefully for five minutes while tossing and turning regularly.

2. Add your garlic and every single one of the finely chopped veggies. Then season with salt and spices to your taste and toss to mix.

3. Cook for up to five to seven minutes on medium-high heat, stirring regularly using a wooden spoon.

4. Add broth, tomatoes, and apricots. Add a little dash of salt again.

5. Keep the heat still on medium-high, cooking for ten more minutes. Then lower the heat and cover the lid. Let it

simmer for a further twenty-five minutes, as the veggies become tender.

6. Add chickpeas, stir and let it cook for five more minutes, still on low heat.

7. Add the lemon juice as well as the fresh parsley. Taste and add more seasoning if necessary. You can also add spices.

8. Move to serving bowls and on each bowl, add toppings of extra virgin olive oil. To be served with couscous, bread, or rice.

MEAL 7: BRIAN

Brian is a traditional Greek roasted vegetable dish with potatoes, zucchini, tomatoes, and red onions with lots of olive oil.

Ingredients

- ✓ Two pounds of peeled and thinly sliced potatoes

- ✓ Four large thinly sliced zucchini

- ✓ Four thinly sliced little red onions

- ✓ Six ripe pureed tomatoes

✓ Two tablespoons of fresh parsley (chopped)

✓ A pinch of sea salt & newly ground black pepper to taste

✓ Half a cup of olive oil

Preparation

1. Preheat the oven to about 400°F (200°C).

2. Spread the potatoes, red onions, zucchinis in a nine-by-thirteen inch of a baking dish, or more preferably. If necessary, you should use two baking dishes.

3. Cover the dish with pureed tomatoes, parsley, and olive oil.

4. Season to your taste with salt and pepper. Mix all ingredients together to achieve even coating.

5. Bake the dish in the preheated oven. After an hour, stir. Don't remove until veggies become tender and the moisture has dried up. This should take around ninety minutes.

6. Let it cool a little before serving or serve at the obtained room temperature.

MEAL 8: GREEK BAKED MEATBALLS +

TOMATO SAUCE

Ingredients

For the Sauce:

- ✓ Half of a minced onion
- ✓ olive oil
- ✓ A clove of garlic
- ✓ Two bay leaves (dried)
- ✓ Five to six pieces of allspice
- ✓ A splash of red wine
- ✓ Three tablespoons of tomato paste
- ✓ Four hundred grams (14 oz) of diced canned tomatoes
- ✓ Half of a teaspoon sugar
- ✓ One teaspoon of ground cumin
- ✓ salt and pepper

For the Meatballs:

- ✓ 800 grams ground beef

- ✓ 1/2 onion minced

- ✓ 3 garlic cloves coarsely chopped

- ✓ 2 tablespoons olive oil

- ✓ 1 egg

- ✓ 5 tablespoons finely ground breadcrumbs or 150 grams (5.3 oz) crustless bread soaked in water

- ✓ A handful of fresh parsley chopped

- ✓ 1 cup water (skip this if using the soaked bread)

- ✓ Salt and pepper

Preparation

For the Sauce:

1. Heat a nice splash of your olive oil inside your cooking pot. This should be done over high heat.

2. Caramelize the garlic and onions.

3. Pour the wine, join it with the spice as well as the bay leaves. Wait till the wine disappears completely from the atmosphere.

4. Add the canned and the tomato paste. Let it cook for a minute or two, while you stir consistently with a wooden spoon.

5. From high, lower the heat to medium. Pour in four cups of water, seasoning (salt & pepper), cumin, and sugar.

6. Cover partly and let it simmer for up to thirty or forty minutes.

For the Meatballs:

1. Preheat the oven to 200°C (392°F.)

2. Combine all ingredients for the meatballs in one mixing bowl.

3. For everything to integrate and interact well, you have to knead the mixture for a couple of minutes. It should have a moist and soft feeling, but still firm enough to be made into shapes. If not, add some more water.

4. Divide the mix into up to 14 parts. Make each part into a round ball with an oval face. Find a baking dish or saucepan that is deep enough to contain the sauce too.

5. Once all the meatballs are safely in the baking dish or pan, use a ladle to pour the sauce on its top. Then bake for forty to fifty minutes, making sure to flip the meatballs so the cooking can be even.

6. Serve

You may serve this dish with potatoes, pasta, or rice. You can add freshly chopped parsley or toasted pine nuts on top, or even red pepper flakes and Greek yogurt.

MEAL 9: SPANISH TUNA AND POTATO SALAD

Ingredients

- ✓ Small red potatoes or fingerling potatoes (12 oz)

- ✓ Trimmed green beans, French (10 oz)

- ✓ Small tomatoes (like Roma or Campari tomatoes) cut into wedges (6 oz)

- ✓ A third of a cup of pearl red onions or quartered small shallots.

✓ A can of excellent tuna (15 oz)

✓ Two or three large cloves of minced garlic

✓ Pepper and salt.

✓ A teaspoon of smoked paprika, or more if you prefer.

✓ Three-quarters of a teaspoon of cumin

✓ Half a teaspoon of crushed red pepper flakes

✓ A third of a cup of virgin olive oil

✓ Three tablespoons of white wine vinegar

✓ Butter lettuce or spring greens (6 oz)

Preparation

1. Put the fingerling tomatoes in a big pot and add water till they're well submerged. Boil for about ten minutes. By then, you should able to push a fork into each potato.

2. Use a slotted spoon to remove the tomatoes from the boiling water and extract it to a plate in the meantime. Don't throw away the water.

3. Set a big bowl beside the pot and fill it with iced water.

4. Add green beans to the cooking pot, with the water at boiling point. Cook for about four minutes.

5. Drain the beans and transfer into the iced water bowl. This will make sure the beans stop cooking and maintain their green color. As soon as it is cool enough, remove the beans from the iced water bowl and pat dry.

6. Cut the fingerlings into equal halves. Put them inside a large mixing bowl and add the green beans, onions/shallots, garlic, and tomatoes. Crumple the tuna up a little before adding it also.

7. Season to taste with pepper, salt, cumin, paprika, and crushed red pepper.

8. Mix vinegar and EVOO and then add it to the salad. Then gently toss everything and ensure all the ingredients coat properly. Taste and decide if you need to add more cumin, paprika, red pepper.

9. Place the butter lettuce or spring greens on a platter and line up the salad on top of it.

10. Serve.

MEAL 10: SAUTEED SHRIMP AND ZUCCHINI

Ingredients

- ✓ One and a half tablespoons of dry oregano

- ✓ A teaspoon of ground cumin

- ✓ A teaspoon of ground coriander

- ✓ Half a teaspoon of sweet paprika

- ✓ An lb of large, peeled, and deveined shrimps (prawns)

- ✓ Olive oil (extra virgin)

- ✓ Half a clove of a medium red onion sliced thinly

- ✓ Five cloves of minced and decided garlic.

- ✓ A piece of bell pepper, cored and neatly sliced into sticks.

- ✓ One or two zucchinis halved lengthways and sliced into a half-moon. You can alternatively use one zucchini and one yellow squash.

- ✓ A cup of drained, cooked chickpeas (from canned chickpeas)

- ✓ One and a half cups of halved cherry tomatoes,

- ✓ Pepper and Kosher salt.

✓ Juice extracted from a large lemon.

✓ A handful of freshly plucked basil leaves, sliced or torn into ribbons. Alternatively, if you can't get basil, you can use a different herb available to you.

Preparation

1. Combine all your spices (cumin, oregano, paprika, and coriander) in a small bowl.

2. Pat the prawns dry and season with the kosher salt and one and half a teaspoon of the spice mix. Set aside for a while or refrigerate till later. What's left of the spice mix is for veggies.

3. Over medium heat, put two tablespoons of extra virgin olive oil in a large skillet. Add your onions and half the total amount of garlic. Cook for about two to three minutes, tossing from time to time fragrant is achieved. However, be careful not to burn the garlic.

4. Add the chickpeas, zucchinis, and bell peppers. Add salt and what's left of the spice mixture. Toss, to allow all the

ingredients to combine well. If there's any need for it, increase the heat just a little bit and cook, tossing from time to time for about five to seven minutes. It's done when the veggies are tender.

5. In the meantime, move the veggies to a large plate. Put the skillet back on the heat and add some more olive oil. Add what's left of the garlic and the seasoned shrimp. Cook at medium-high heat and frequently stir until the shrimp turns pink. This should take about four-or five-minutes tops.

6. Put the already cooked veggies back into the skillet, as well as the shrimps. Add the lemon juice and cherry tomatoes. Toss everything together and finish by adding the fresh basil as garnish.

7. Try not to overcook the shrimps. Large shrimps cook in no time, so you need to be watchful. Once the thickest part goes from grey to pink, the cooking is enough. Depending on the pan's shrimp size and quantity, it should normally take four to five minutes.

MEDITERRANEAN DIET: AN ENJOYABLE WAY TO LOSE WEIGHT WITHOUT RESTRICTIONS

THE MEDITERRANEAN DIET FOR BEGINNERS

The Mediterranean diet strongly encourages eating a wide array of nutrient-rich foods and places a healthy restriction on the consumption of processed foods and added sugars, which are, more often than not, calorie high. Due to this reason, you could ensure weight loss by pairing the Mediterranean diet with a strong and healthy lifestyle.

For a long time, the diet has been known for being of major benefit to the heart. More recently, it has also been revealed that the diet boosts brain activity and that that it is also super effective both for losing and maintaining weight, especially among older adults.

The Mediterranean diet also encourages people to take up eating patterns that are have predominantly made of fruits and vegetables, whole grains, and healthy fats. (nuts, fish, and seafood).

But several diets come with the same or similar benefits.

THE MEDITERRANEAN DIET FOR BEGINNERS

So, these are the components that actually make the Mediterranean diet unique, as well as many quick suggestions to make the diet work out well for you:

- ✓ The Mediterranean diet promotes physical exercise.
- ✓ It steers you away from the excessive consumption of heavily processed foods.
- ✓ It works just well.

It has been found that those who follow the diet over extended periods get to experience healthy weight loss, heart improvement, and lowered risk of developing some types of cancer.

HOW TO MAKE THE MEDITERRANEAN DIET

WORK FOR YOU

1. Start Slow.

Factually, a healthy diet is about breaking up old negative habits and replacing them with new and positive ones. The easiest way to get it all wrong, it to deprive yourself of everything you've been used to in such a short time.

Introduce new foods or fitness routine slowly but gradually, over the first couple of weeks. This will give your body and your mind the needed time to adjust to the new lifestyle.

2. Eat A Variety of Foods.

Another huge mistake many people make when trying to incorporate a new diet — even that works — is repeating the same three meals per day every single day. It just makes the whole thing boring.

A good combination of different veggies and fruits, whole grains, and proteins at every meal will also help quench hunger faster. This is very helpful where portion control and avoiding extra calories are concerned.

3. Choose Fitness Activities You Love.

If you don't like the idea of working out for 150 minutes every week, it will be difficult to keep going. Like you do your meals, switch up your gym life too. Don't be boring.

While working out the array of muscle groups in your body, do or find something to keep you entertained.

It might just be that we're looking at this whole thing from the wrong perspective. Dieting should not just be about food restrictions or losing that extra ten pounds by over-exercising. It is more about figuring out how to prepare and enjoy good food and make interesting physical work outs happen.

CONCLUSION

THE MEDITERRANEAN DIET FOR BEGINNERS

There are many reasons for the recent selection by the United States News and World Report of the Mediterranean diet as the most ranked of the over 40 globally recognized diets they took a look at. The nice thing about the Mediterranean diet is that, compared with other diet plans, it doesn't focus on eliminations or restrictions. Instead, it uses a more inclusive approach. You can adopt the Mediterranean diet and lifestyle and not get to really experience that feeling of missing out on all the nice foods and flavors of this world.

There is a certain emphasis on balance, portion control, making the best lifestyle choices, and eating really good, healthy food. The diet is more about portion control, balance, and making good choices in eating more real good real food.

As illustrated by the pyramid below, there's a lot of focus on fruits, beans, veggies, nuts, legumes, all at the base of the pyramid. Then at the top of the pyramid, we have lean proteins from poultry and fish, healthy fats from olive oil, dairy, even consuming some sweets and red meats on rarer occasions.

How to Follow the Mediterranean Diet:

Advice for Beginners

If you're new to the Mediterranean way of eating, many experts recommend beginning with what is known as "simple swaps."

In the first week, get some really good extra virgin olive oil and resolve to adopt olive oil, in place of lard, butter, and other oils, as your go-to cooking oil.

For the second week, smuggle two seafood-based meals into your diet. You could also do a meatless meal or two during the same week. Get some healthy snacks like veggies, dried or fresh fruits, or even hummus.

To conclude your meals, you could introduce, in place of desserts, locally produced cheese like Pecorino, Fetta Romano, Parmigiano, etc. Also, you can enjoy the likes of cherries, figs, or dried apricots.

Generally, you should not rush anything. Take it one step at a time and try to get your body used to the lifestyle and diet. It will also help if you have loved ones or friends who are willing to go with you on this journey. It makes it feel not like a lonely road to walk.

If you have underlying health conditions, it is advisable to consult with your doctor and talk this over to see their recommendations.

Remember, the Mediterranean diet isn't just about what you eat; it is also about eating it. So, incorporate physical activities and food sharing into your routines.

Good luck on the journey!

CPSIA information can be obtained
at www.ICGtesting.com
Printed in the USA
LVHW090149081121
702727LV00006B/143

9 781801 572255